Jordan got the bus to Gran and Grandad's.

He saw a kid in a wheelchair getting on and moaned as she took so long.

He sighed when he had to wait for a man with a stick.

BUS
STOP
42

When he got there, Gran beckoned to him.

“Grandad’s sleeping,” she whispered, “but he needs his saw from the loft. Can you get it?”

Jordan nodded. It was something to do.

There was an odd-looking black hat in the loft, hanging on a hook.

Jordan popped it on.

All of a sudden, he yelled. “Ow! My back hurts and I’ve got pains in my leg.”

When he saw himself, he had a shock. His hair and whiskers were just like Grandad’s!

“How can this be?” he muttered.

Jordan crept out of Gran and Grandad's. He needed Grandad's stick to help him.

Out in the street, Jordan was astonished. Odd shops had sprung up and the cars were all so quick.

There were lots of jet buses in the air too. They all had Nexajet on them.

This was not the present!

When Jordan took the hat off, he was right back in his Gran and Grandad's loft. His back and legs no longer hurt.

"Now I understand what it's like to be 80," he said.

“Grandad,” said Jordan. “When I was in the loft ... ”

“The hat?” said Grandad with a grin. “What did you gain from what happened?”

Jordan was astonished. “I need to be understanding,” he said.

“Never forget that,” said Grandad. “It’s so important.”

Jordan got the bus back to his mom and dad's apartment. He saw the kid in the wheelchair, but now he grinned and helped her.

Then he saw what was on the wheelchair.

Nexajet!

Back at the apartment, Jordan checked for Nexajet. It was a little start-up that did wheelchairs.

"It will not be like that for long!" said Jordan. "I shall invest cash in Nexajet now. Then, in years to come, my back and legs might hurt – but I will be rich!"

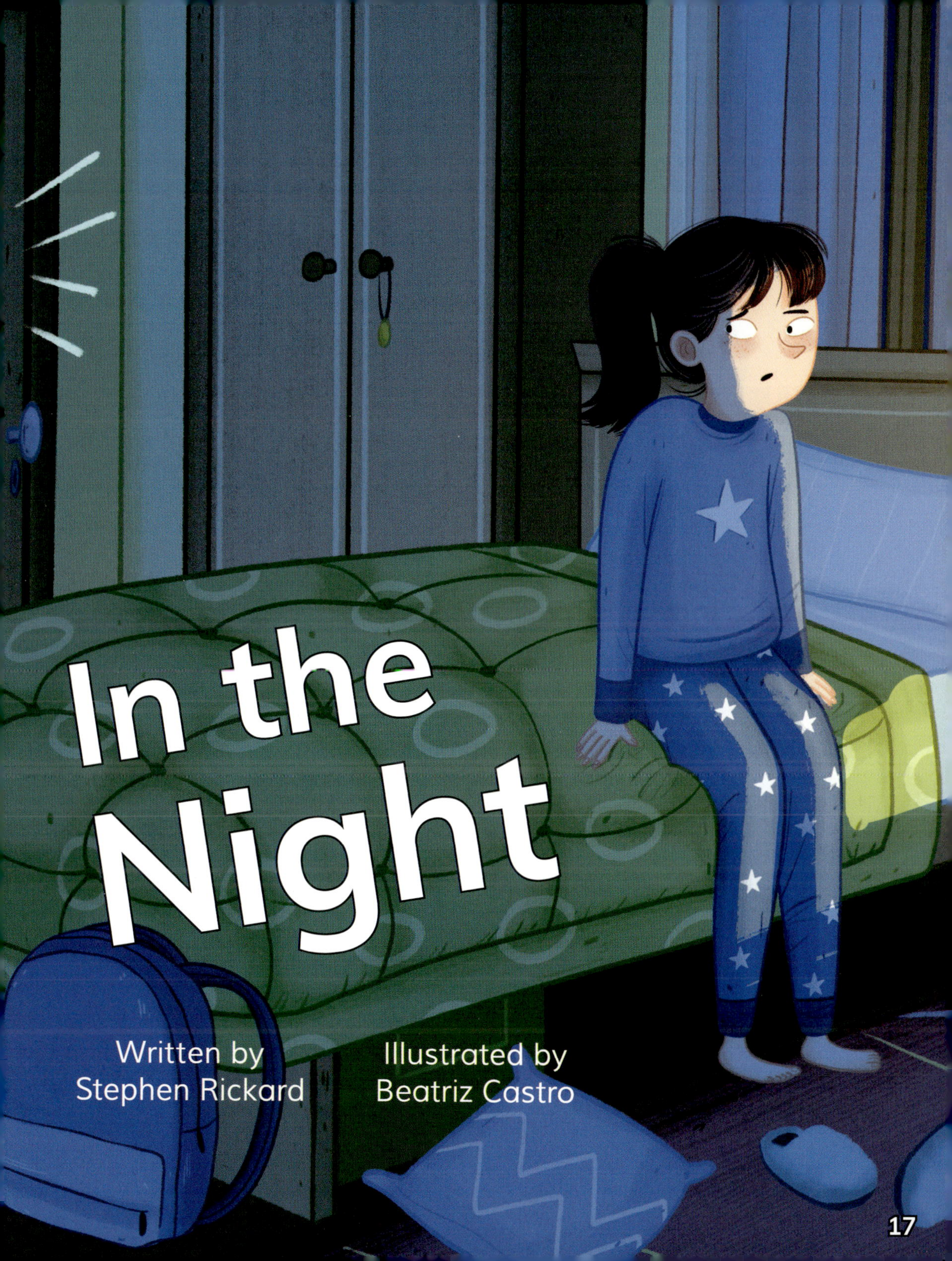

In the Night

Written by
Stephen Rickard

Illustrated by
Beatriz Castro

Philippa was upset. Andrew was yelling in the bedroom next to hers.

"Dark night ... coward ... madness ... darkness ... " he yelled.

Then he added, "This weekend!"

The yelling went on and on. It was hard not to hear it.

This had been happening for some weeks now.

Andrew was Philippa's twin.
They got on well, but this was grim.

What was Andrew up to?

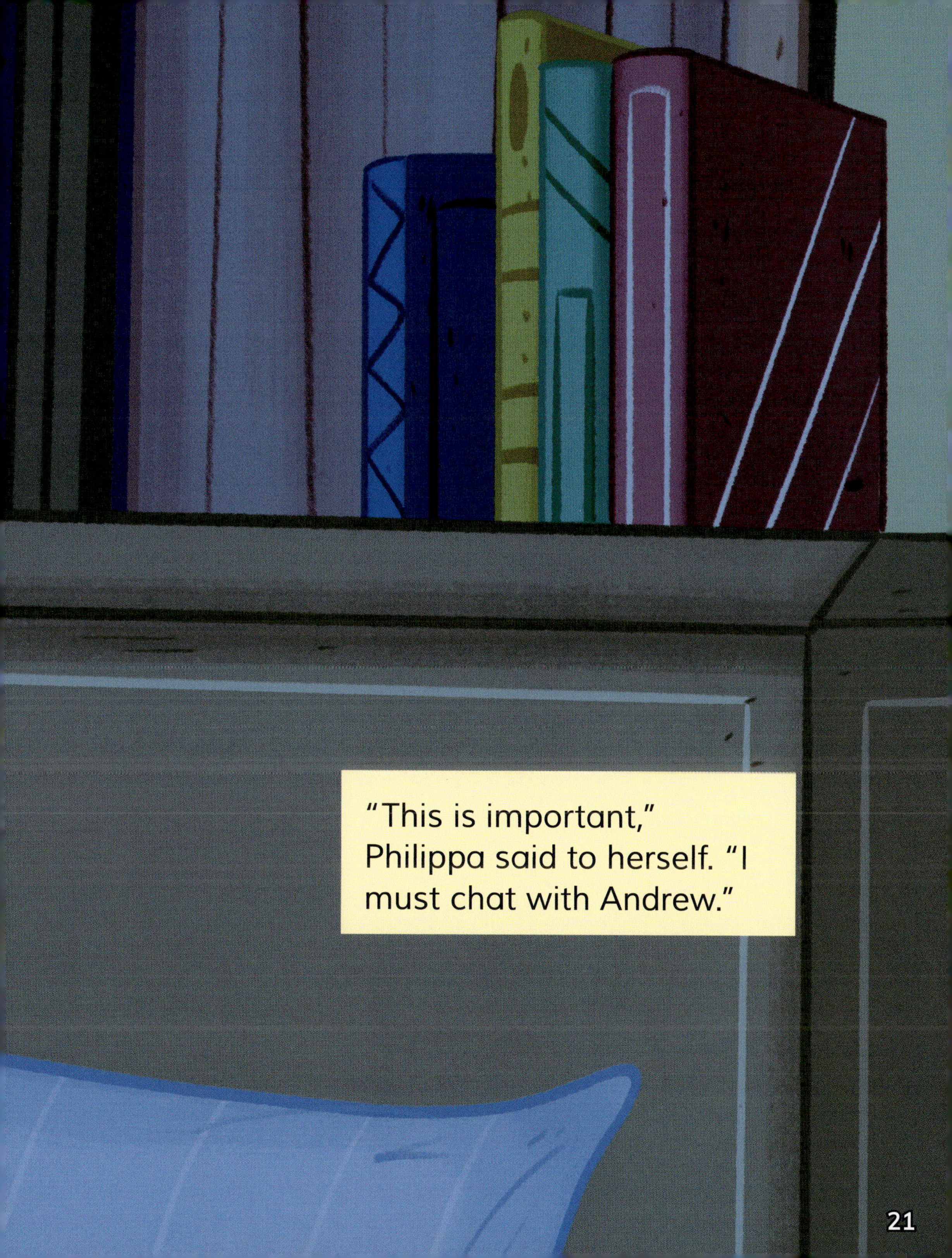

"This is important," Philippa said to herself. "I must chat with Andrew."

In the morning, Philippa sat down with Andrew.

"What is happening, Andrew?" she said. "I can hear you in the night."

Andrew just shrugged and left the room.

So Philippa met Yasha for a coffee. She explained to Yasha what Andrew had said in his room that night.

"It might be something bad," said Yasha. "You need to go to an adult. To start, you might tell Mom."

Philippa did not go to her mom – not just yet.

Philippa liked running, and she trained at the track in town. So she met up with her trainer, Beth Wiggins.

She explained to Beth what Andrew had been doing.

"My husband Bob helps kids with problems," Beth said. "That's his job – and he's good at it. Let's all meet – Mom, Dad, you, me, and Bob."

So Mr. and Mrs. Wiggins had a meeting with Philippa and her mom and dad. Andrew was not there.

Philippa explained what had been happening.

"This is all a bit shocking," said Dad with a sigh. "I will go and get Andrew. Then we can chat to him."

So Andrew, Philippa, Mom, Dad and Mr. and Mrs. Wiggins all ended up sitting in the living room.

Andrew was a bit flustered.

"Look, Andrew," said Dad. "At night, Philippa can hear you yelling. You said upsetting things, like 'cowards' and 'darkness.' What is going on?"

All of a sudden, Andrew grinned from ear to ear. Then he snorted with glee.

"Ha! It's no problem – it's not something bad. I have joined an acting club. I am going to star as Macbeth – so, at night, you can just hear me practicing my part!"

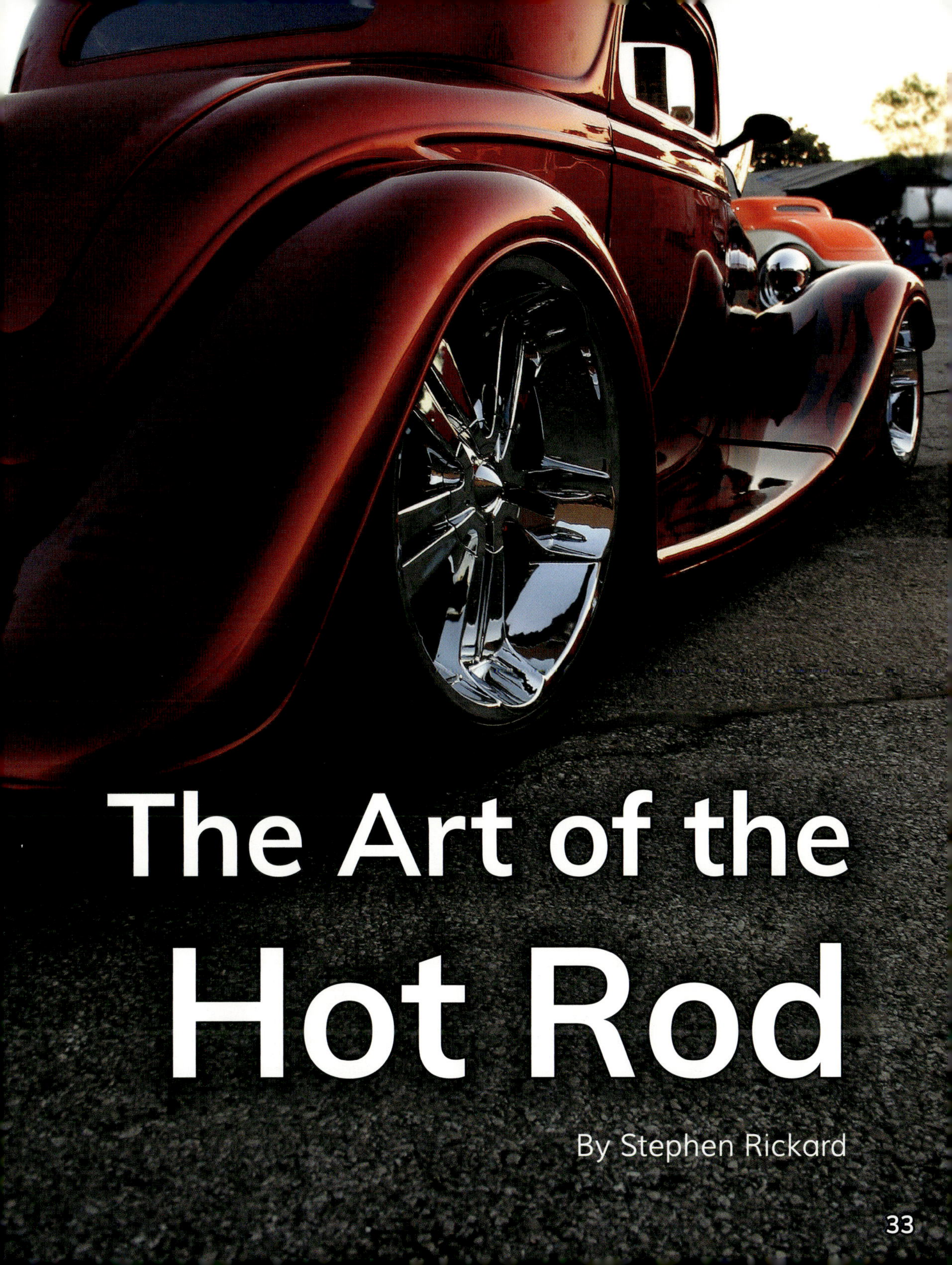

The Art of the Hot Rod

By Stephen Rickard

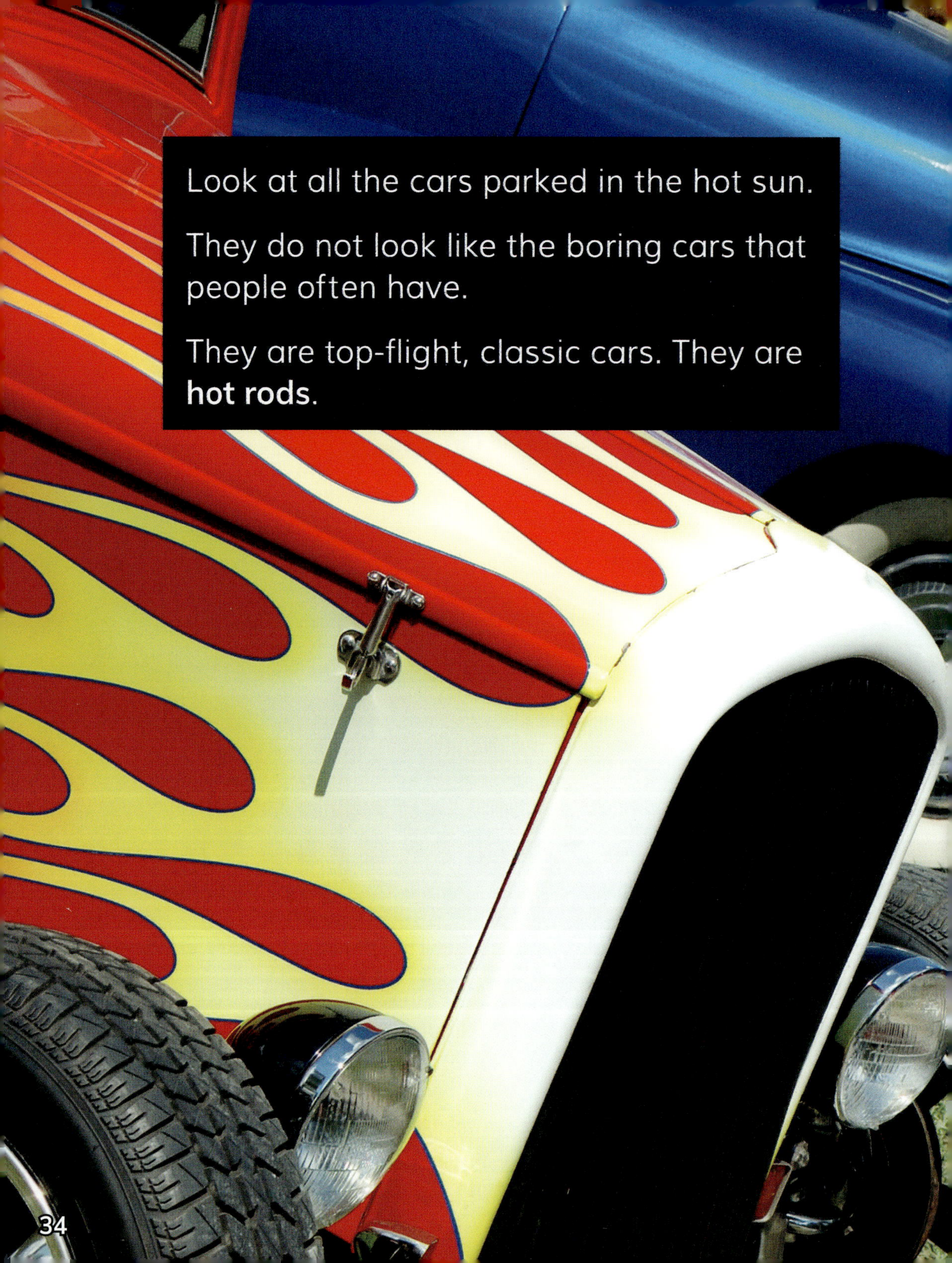

Look at all the cars parked in the hot sun.

They do not look like the boring cars that people often have.

They are top-flight, classic cars. They are **hot rods**.

Hot rods started in America in the 1930s.

Then the trend blew up and, in a flash, the numbers grew.

Hot rods are cars that are set up to be quick, with loads of extra power.

Just look at the wheels on this car.

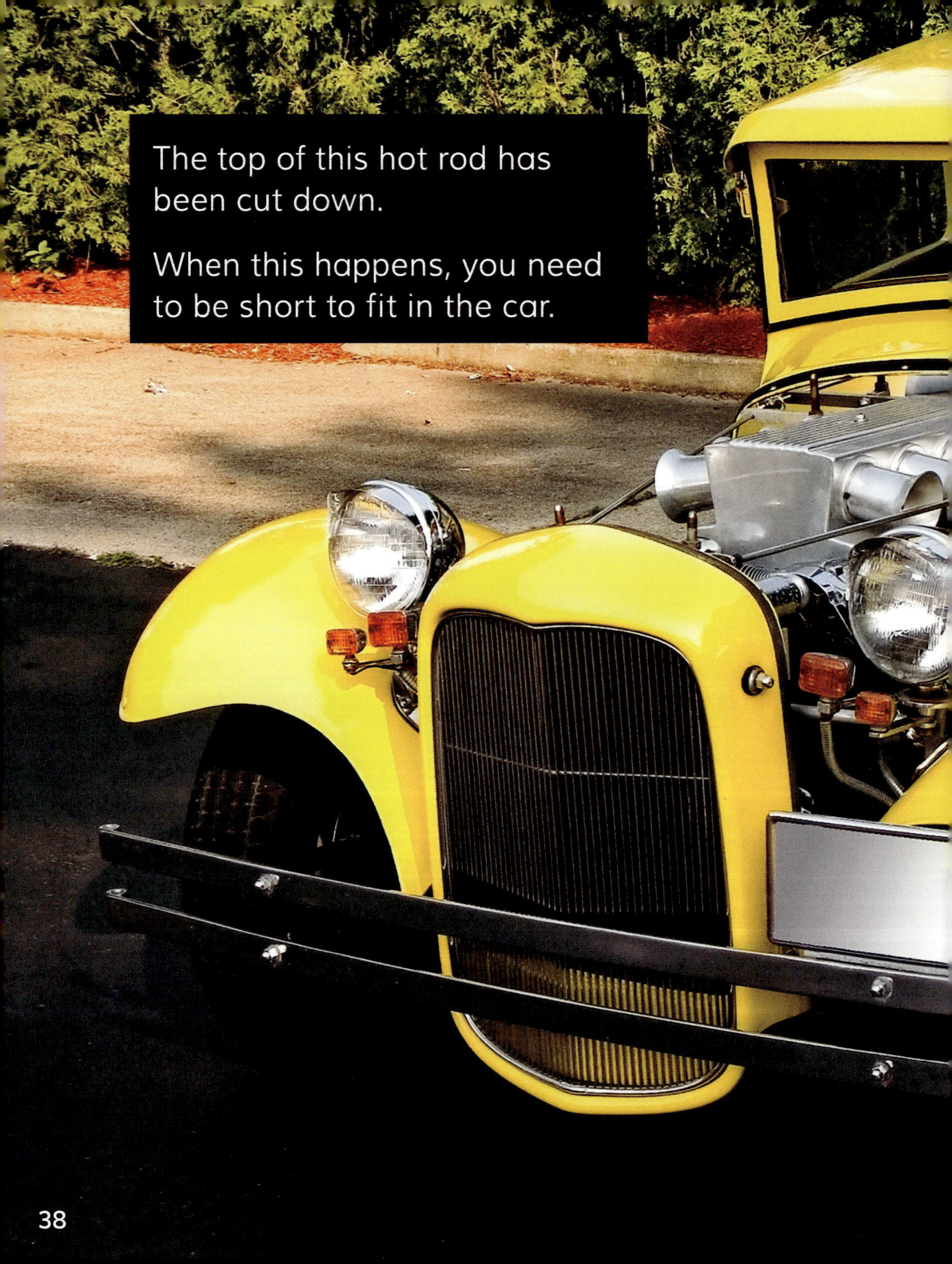

The top of this hot rod has been cut down.

When this happens, you need to be short to fit in the car.

The cars are bright.

Each car is saying, "Look at me! I am not boring."

Each car has the looks to draw a crowd.

Then, when you go for a trip in it, you will see just how quick it is.

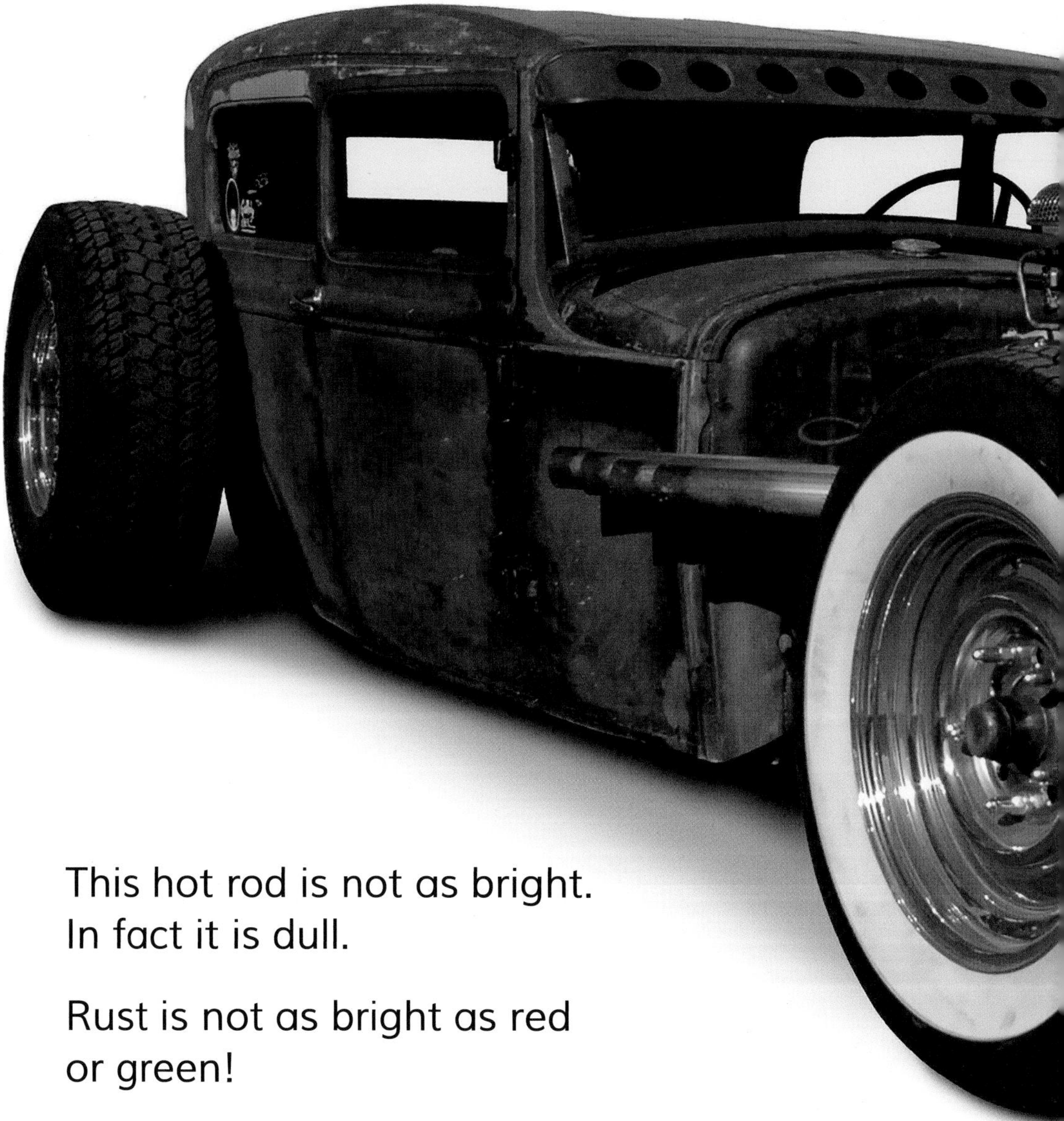

This hot rod is not as bright.
In fact it is dull.

Rust is not as bright as red
or green!

It is a **rat rod**. It is as quick as a hot rod, but it looks raw, as if it is not yet finished.

The flaws are part of its charm.

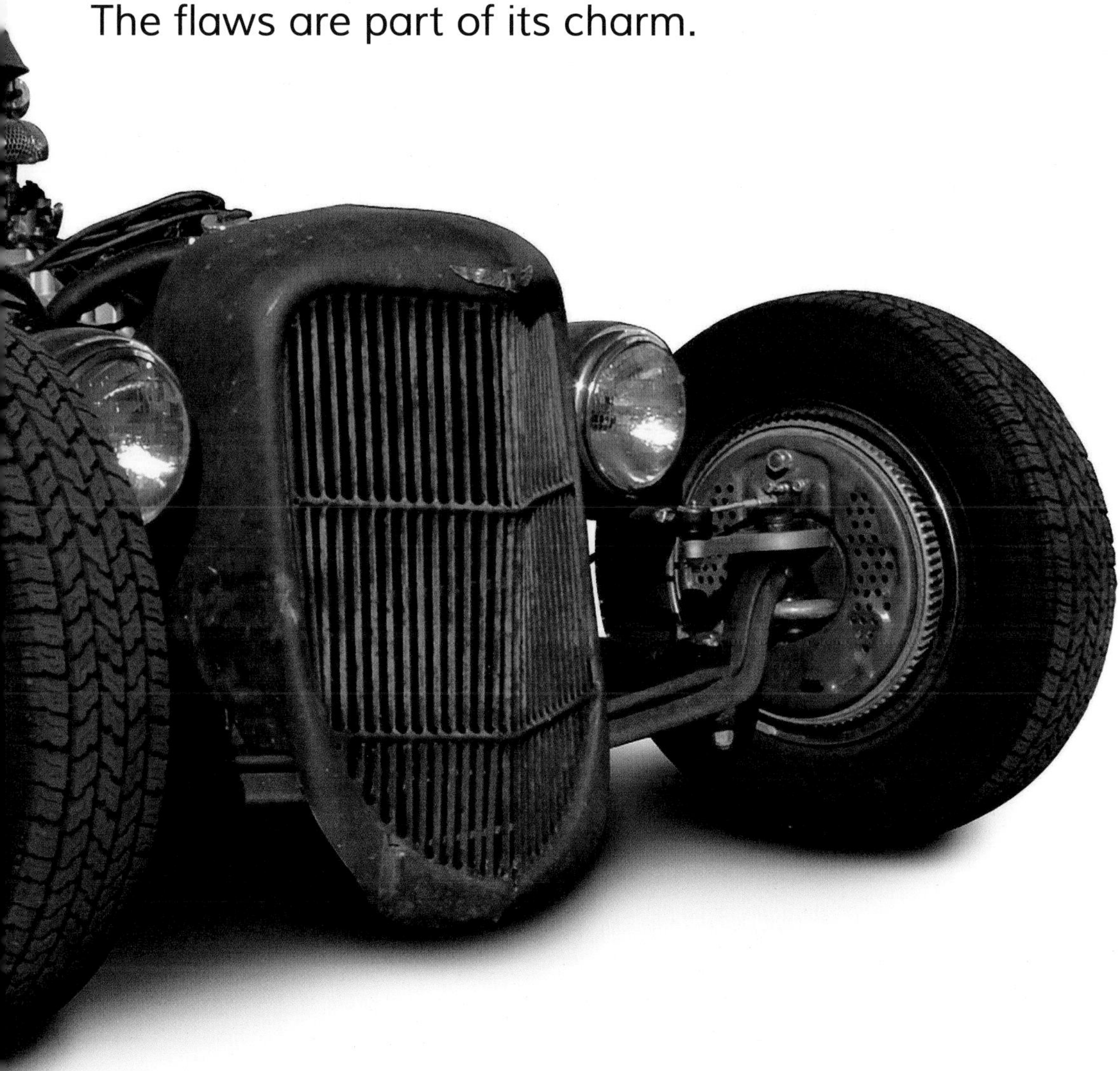

Some hot rods have stunning graphics sprayed on.

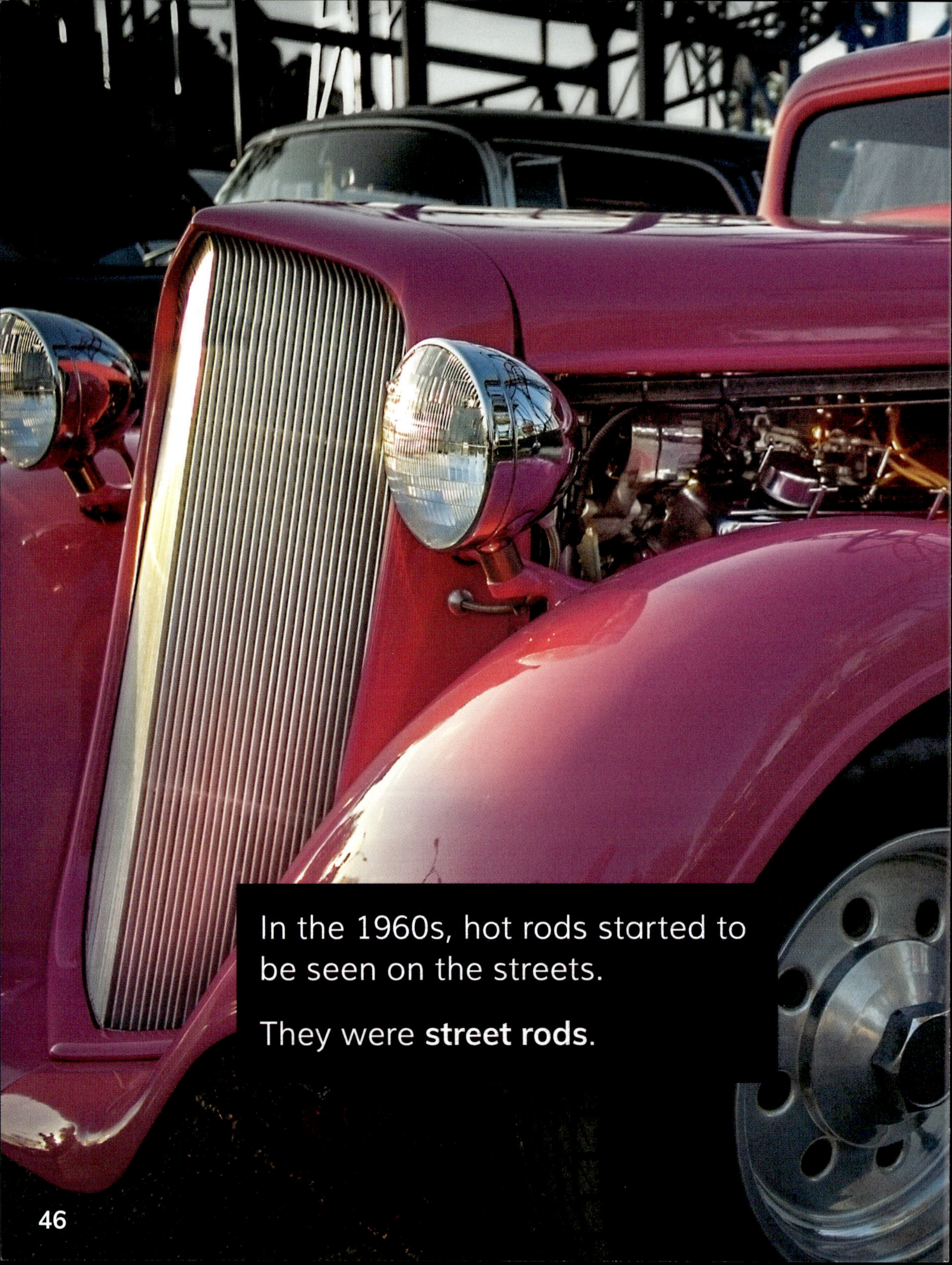

In the 1960s, hot rods started to be seen on the streets.

They were **street rods**.

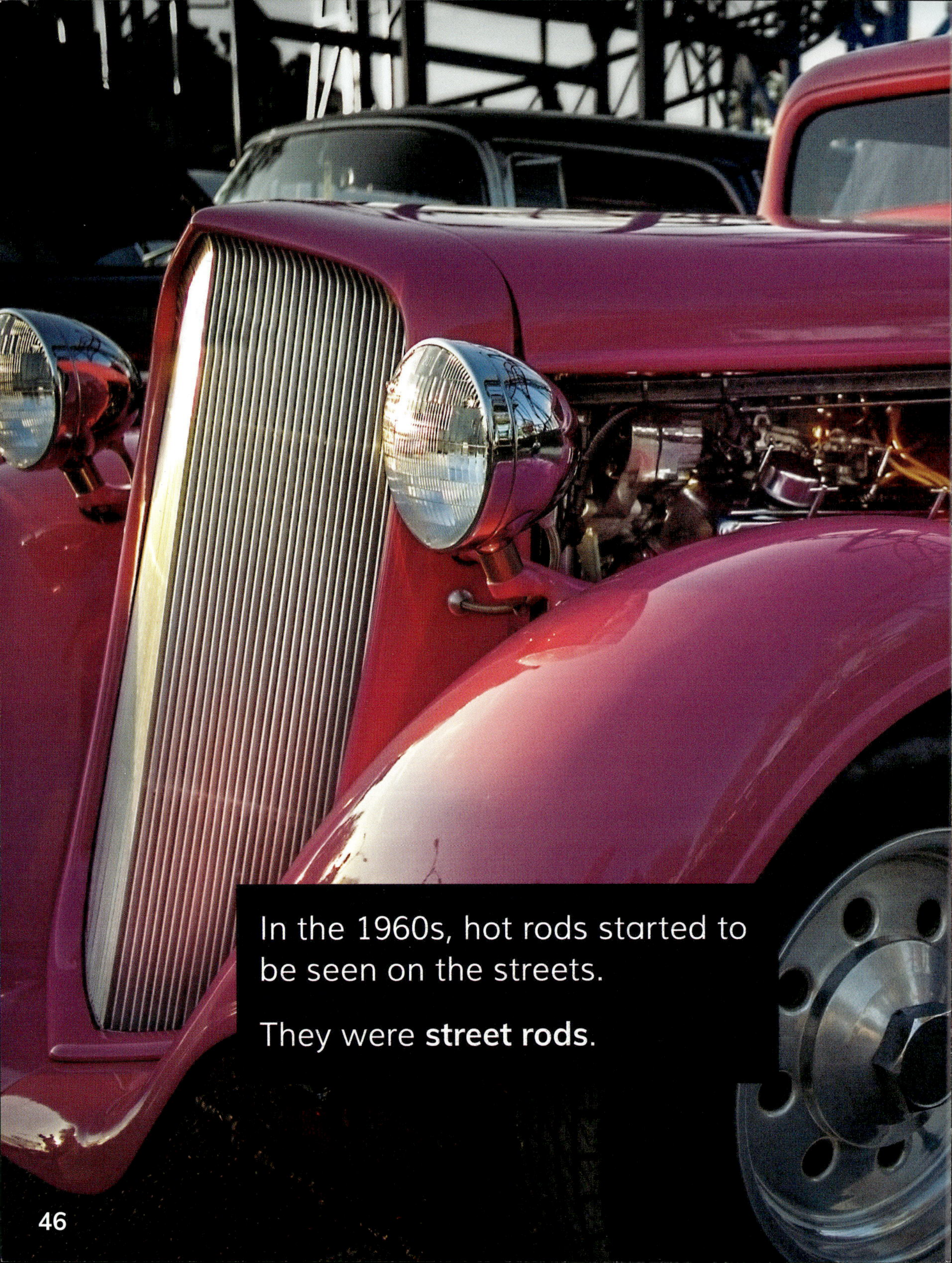

In the 1960s, hot rods started to be seen on the streets.

They were **street rods**.

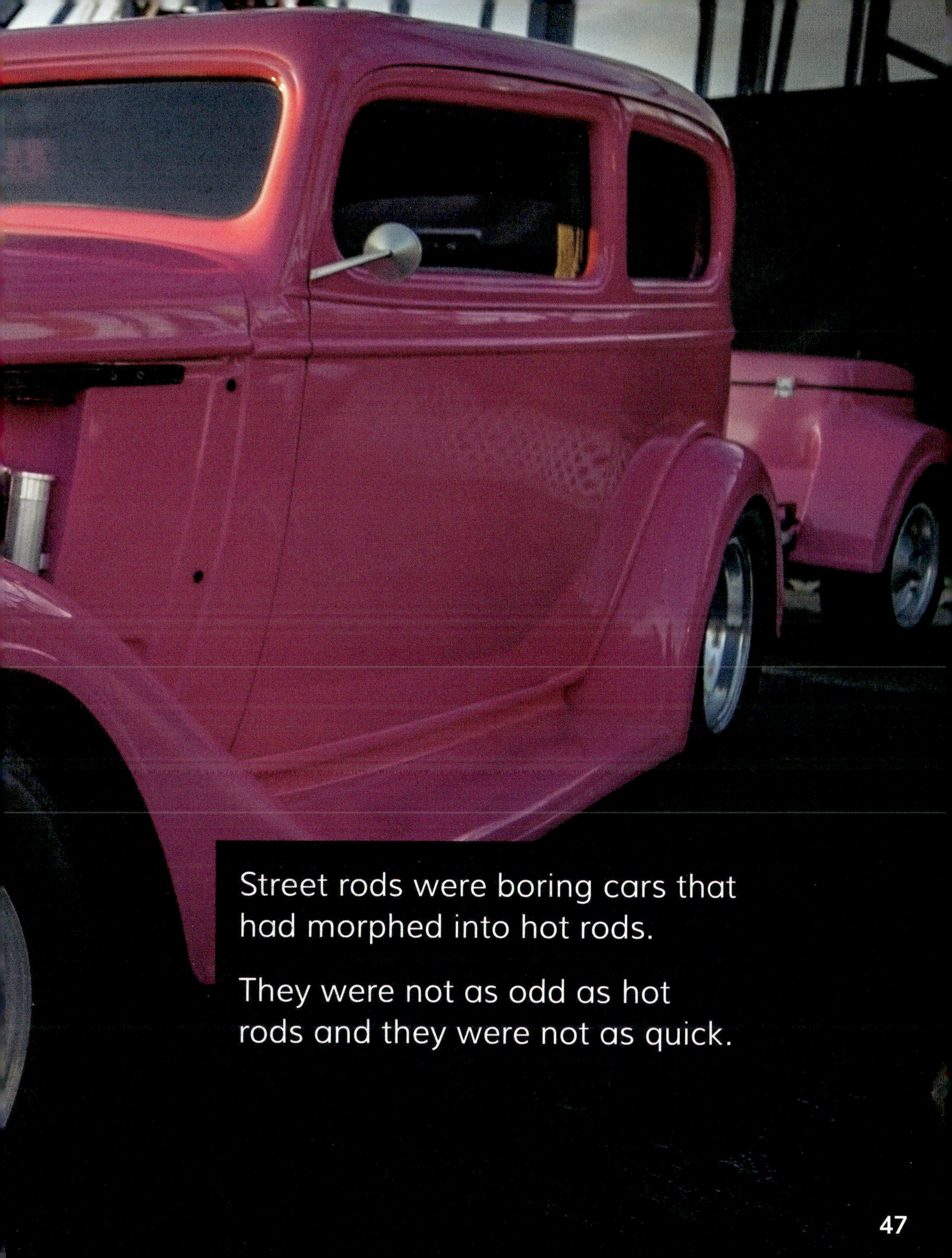

Street rods were boring cars that had morphed into hot rods.

They were not as odd as hot rods and they were not as quick.

Little kids can have hot rods too. Ben and Tom Baxter have constructed their first rat rod.

I reckon Mr. and Mrs. Baxter will be so proud.

The Hat

Written by
Jill Atkins

Illustrated by
Ma Pe

Published in 2026 by
Norwood House Press
2544 Clinton Street
Buffalo, NY 14224

Printed in the United States of America

Library of Congress Cataloging-in-Publication Data:
Names: Atkins, Jill (Children's author). | Rickard, Stephen, 1957-, author. | Pe, Ma, illustrator. | Castro, Beatriz, illustrator.
Title: The hat / written by Jill Atkins, illustrated by Ma Pe. In the night / written by Stephen Rickard, illustrated by Beatriz Castro. The art of the hot rod / written by Stephen Rickard.
Description: Buffalo, NY : Norwood House Press, 2026. | Series: Phonics all-stars: phase 5a
Identifiers: ISBN 9781978578982 (pbk.) | ISBN 9781978578999 (library bound) | ISBN 9781978579002 (ebook)
Subjects: LCSH: Reading–Phonetic method–Juvenile fiction. | English language–Phonetics–Juvenile fiction. | Children and older people–Juvenile fiction. | Twins–Juvenile fiction. | Families–Juvenile fiction. | Automobile racing–Juvenile fiction.
Classification: LCC LB1573.3 A796 2026 | DDC 372.465–dc23

CPSIA compliance information: Batch #CW26NHP: For further information contact Norwood House Press at 1-800-237-9932.

"Go and see Gran and Grandad this weekend," said Dad. "They like seeing you."

Jordan yawned.

"It's so boring there," he said. "Grandad nods off and Gran just likes her jigsaws."

"We all end up like that," said Dad with a grin.